Home

Jade Anna Hughes

FOR MEG
WHOSE WORDS ALWAYS GIVE ME REASON TO BELIEVE IN MYSELF

CONTENTS

"The ache for home lives in all of us, the safe place where we can go as we are and not be questioned." – Maya Angelou

Where is Home

I

Where is home? I don't know, it has changed so many times over the years. Sometimes it changes over the space of a day. You know, home is here, or home is there. Home is everywhere! But where is home really? I spent many years wondering this, yearning for somewhere else, nostalgic, homesickness just another part of my everyday emotional pool. I put my hands in, try to wash it away but there she is, wrapped around the reflection of the New York skyline or the Vercors mountain range. I close my eyes and there it is, my old boulangerie, the smell of freshly baked baguette right there in my nose. Or sometimes it is the bar on Orchard Street, the sounds in the walls when you walk through the doors, cool air, dried glass rings, the comforting smell of old beer that never goes away. Other times it is the churchyard in England, moss-covered tombstones, and names that have long since been forgotten by most. And then I imagine myself walking barefoot down the hill to the little beach on the Mediterranean, a mile or so from Nahariya, a few more from Akko. Home was leaving one home and landing in another, even when I had never been there before. Home was a suitcase in one hand and a cigarette in another, $200 in a bank account and a new life wherever I laid my head. Home is and will always be where I feel safe, happy, and with those I love.

II Birth

The smell of rain on the warm pavement in the middle of the summer, a couple of swallows flying for cover into the eaves above my bedroom window, and the sound of the breeze rustling through branches and leaves, that is home. England in the summertime is home. Right there in the village where there is one main road and a few smaller ones, and two churches, the bells ringing on Sundays in time for the morning service. England is also the little room at the top of the building, with the grand staircase leading down to the rest of the apartment, cooking smells coming from the kitchen, the fire crackling in the living room. Home is the warm, thick quilt on Nana's bed, watching television in the evening because I was allowed to stay up later than my sister. England is also living in London on next to nothing, writing poetry on my lunch break in Putney by the river; dreaming of Israel and California while wandering through the streets of Streatham. England is my first home, the home where I was born, and where I have returned to many a time. England is the comfort, the warmth, but also the grey and the dark. England is living as a working class family under Thatcher in the 80's, but England is also rolling hills of green beauty and old, old pubs with real ale.

III Becoming

The unseasonably warm breeze cutting through the November air, leaves falling red, yellow, brown to the ground, but still t-shirt weather when yesterday we were in winter coats. Home is the Mistral whistling through the mountains into the valley, a city where the blue sky is tainted by brown pollution, nestled down between different mountain ranges. Vercors, Chartreuse, Belledonne: that is where I am from. France is nights spent sitting on the statue of Berlioz singing songs with a bottle of rosé in my hands; hand in hand with my best friend, running through the cobbled streets causing havoc. Home is ivresse, home is warm bread and brie, ravioles baked in the oven, and countless espressos sitting outside en terrasse, no matter how hot or cold it is. Home is the relentless heat in the summer, and the snowcapped mountains in the winter. Home is opening your window shutters every morning to be greeted by the foot of a mountain, looming up into the sky, faces in the rocks, trees that turn with the seasons, somewhat oppressing, mostly a safety blanket. Never a real sunset on the horizon, sometimes I missed that, but those beautifully dramatic thunderstorms made up for it twice over. Dancing in the rain, happy faces, a kind of freedom from everything. Home is teenage years and metal and grunge and goth and friendships that last forever. Home is the most beautiful language in the world.

IV Believing

The smell of 5am in the spring, early morning jogger passing late night last caller, city that never sleeps: that is home. New York City, the place where so many dreams go to die, where so many dreams go to shine, is my home. A decade of decadence, a decade of wonder, of ups and downs and squiggly all arounds: a home that I never expected, but the home that I always craved. So many boots worn into the ground, uptown, downtown, Brooklyn, Queens, bridges and tunnels and subways and ferries. I can still find my way there blindfolded, the city sounds music to my ears. City sounds at night put me to sleep now, silence keeps me awake, ears craving the soothing sounds of sirens and cars, loud beats and voices travelling below my window. Home is the smell of laundry, bakery, trash, and stale beer all on the same block. Home is where love waxed and waned, and finally fell straight. Home is where my daughters were born, where the eldest took her first steps, and where life took a different turn. New York

City: city where I lost and found myself over and over again, falling, crawling, standing up and walking tall. Home that haunts my dreams and my daydreams. Homesickness is the strongest with this one.

V Family

And now, home is here in this little city, capital of such a big state. Boiling hot in the summer, damp in the winter, wedged between desert and mountain, I suppose it is home. Home because we have a home, and home because my family is here. I still wander the streets like a stranger, one foot on, one foot off; looking for places we can make our own. We live in the bustle, but it is quiet, and we walk everywhere, every day. Past the Capitol where laws are passed and protests are held, through the gardens where each tree proudly displays a name and a history, up, up towards the real bustle, figuring out where we belong. I have known Sacramento on and off for 17 years and she appears to be struggling. Growing, but not fast enough, streets a mess of new and tumbledown, not enough room for the residents, K Street an image of the US that no one wants the world to see. Old Sacramento has my heart; the rumble of the wooden sidewalks as the stroller rolls over the slats, Evangeline's beckoning us inside, memories of centuries lingering in the alleyways. I learn to love you, new home, the place where my son was born, but we will not be staying, our plans have many more horizons ahead of them.

VI Heart

Laced in between those homes are other homes, temporary stays that became more permanent, and forever etched into my mind. Barefoot walks to the edge of the moshav, running around the kibbutz at night... The little house in the suburbs, the place where I learnt what prejudice really meant, being spat on because I wasn't blonde and didn't speak Dutch. Biking to school, rain or shine, learning a new language in the space of weeks, months, little brains like sponges, watching, absorbing, listening. I still smell the Prasad in India, the overpowering smell of flowers on the tomb in the early morning, a perfect quiet, no one to bother me while I wrote and sketched. Sterilized water in containers outside of the rooms, perfectly crafted vegetarian meals, and people from all walks of life, a moment in time, ships passing through the night. That balcony in Barcelona, summer moon shining through my cigarette smoke as I listened to Cat Stevens and dreamed about coming back home, because those streets reminded me of home, of France home. My life is formed by a pattern of homes, all tracing backwards and forwards, down hills, over mountains, with many, many flights between them.

VII

One day we will make our home somewhere else again. Another country, maybe one I have never resided in before, maybe one that I already call home. The wind has a tendency to turn and cast me off into all types of directions, heart first, the rest following right behind. If there is one thing I have learnt it is to never wait for something to happen, instead one should grab ahold of it and not let go.

Freedom Butterflies

I ran 5 miles, and then walked 6 more.
Something happened on the bridge
The sky was grey, droplets of humid air
Falling on my sweaty face.
That song started in my ears, guitars flowing,
I looked up and saw them:
Black butterflies, a horde of them,
Over my head, over the barriers,
Over to the water, going away.
I felt it then, that complete freedom.
Freedom to breathe, to shout, to cry.
Release. Released it all.
Hunger and strength, heartbreak and joy.
Etched on my skin now. And forever.
Liberté, you set me free. I breathe.
No.
More.
Hiding.

Fly, fly, fly away over the waters to the unknown that is fearless.

Pray away (it won't do any good)

Be quiet. No one needs to hear your voice.
Go away. No one needs to see your face.
Get downstairs. I have something to tell you.
I love you. Don't you know that?
Shut up. I have something to tell you.
Stop your bloody crying! It's too late.
Wear this beautiful dress, not those jeans.
Tie your hair back, it's much too long.
Be quiet. Be quiet and pray.
Because we all need saving, all of us.
Recite these poems and pray, pray, pray.
My love is not enough to save us all.
Pour me another glass, switch the record over.
Silence. I need to hear my thoughts.
No one needs to hear yours.

And then there was silence.

No more shouting, no more crying.
No more hitting, no more sadness.
No more pain, no more praying, no more fear.

Oh, of course, it wasn't all bad, was it?
Times of happiness, not all has disappeared.
It's just that the deepest scars are the ones that never really go away.

One day I will paint you in black, white and red,
And my voice will sing for you from the rooftops of this city.

My vision is just not your perspective.

Paternal Instinct

"I've left a present for you upstairs",
Hanging in a doorway from the
Dirty brown wooden beam.
Just for you.
To take into your arms
And hug, and pour out your sorrows to.
The butterflies will flutter down
To scoop up what I left behind.
No words, no aimless words,
No comforting scrolling lines, only
A scattering of people who forget,
Who disappear, who won't speak.

Did the eagle pick you up
And take you to its nest, far
Up in the radiant mountain?
Or are you walking through miles
Of greying corridors until someone meets
You, someone like your own self?

Pieces of paper put together will
Never make the puzzle whole again.

Easter Day

Easter Day and in my heart
The orphan feeling releases
It's tangible fingers out again.
Yesterday she gave me an egg,
I gave her one, and we gave
Him an egg. Sweet laughter.
But today: Sunday, lunches
And dinners, family ensemble.
Alone; bread, coffee,
Leftover chocolate.
Day of forgiveness and
Tears smear my outlook
Today, because I want to
Be with those who are far away.
Because sometimes the physical
Touch is the only action that
Takes the pain away.

Tonight

Tonight I blew smoke to the stars,
They smiled down on me,
Twinkle, twinkle, silver shadow,
My bottle sparkled with a grin,
And I twirled around to my song,
Chanel spray in the air,
With girlie girls and tomboys,
We dance and laugh and flirt;
Everything goes tonight
Because I don't care anymore
No I don't care anymore.
I want to be pretty and cute,
But I'm just beautiful and obnoxious.
Freakshow or playground
Whatever you choose;
But whatever you want
I will not be.
Only time will show if we were
Right or wrong
But tell me,
Do sluts go to heaven too?

La rue d'en bas

Curled up in a ball
Silently screaming to end it all
Crying and crying and crying out loud
Threatening to cut myself to pieces
Another line, another shot
Everything is OK again
Dancing on the bar
Singing along to the song
Laughing and laughing and laughing out loud
Loving every minute of it
Another line, another shot
Everything falls apart again

I don't remember what I did last night.

Running through the streets
Hoping to find where I want to be
Shouting and shouting and shouting inside
Wishing I were not here
Another line, another shot
Everything is OK again
Kissing a random stranger
Happy in someone's arms
Smiling and smiling and smiling too much
The wonderful life of the party
Another line, another shot
Everything falls apart again

I don't remember what I did last night.

Unravel the string
Slowly but surely
Until all that is left
Is hopelessness
Black out the nights
Until there is just
A deep hole of nothingness
Lose all cares until
Nothing matters anymore

It's all going to be OK tomorrow
As long as there is
Another line, another shot
Another line, another shot

I don't remember what happened last night.

Same old, same old

5am: drunk swaying dog walk.
6am: tears while staring at the cat.
7am: sleep?
8am: thunder crashes. Awake.
9am: people shouting outside.
10am: text message ping.
10:01am: not from the right person.
10:30am: toilet run.
11am: sleep?
Noon: alarm is going off in 30 mins.
12:10pm: dozing? Cat purring.
12:30pm: alarm.
12:31pm: pounding, pounding headheartache.

Thanks and no thanks for not responding
Again.
One day you want everything.
The next you care for nothing.

1am: sleep.

I have too much to accomplish
In my life
To sit around at home
Feeling like crap.

Barcelona Moon

She's in the same place as last night,
Even brighter.
Time for me to say goodbye,
Yet another place to be nostalgic about,
Yet another moment to store away,
To remember next year and the one after.
Beautiful statues, I hope you see them too
I probably won't ever sit here again
But I will keep this spot in my memory.
The place where I was inspired
To wake up and feel again.
Hope, freedom, love, pain, angst,
Tears, laughter, worry, happiness.
Time to cry, time to laugh,
Thank you special place
I will see you again in a different time.

Paradox

Wall wrapped around the paradox
Brick by brick, built steadily,
One knocked down, two replace it.
Thick, sturdy, heavy, tough.
Chatterbox but deeply quiet.
Paradox protects herself from life.

Paradox is unhappy again.
Kill, kill, kill this feeling.
I dream of more
Egalité, Liberté, Fraternité.

No acceptance.

Autumn

The days draw in on me,
That old feeling of comfort,
Warmth in the cold.
Hot teas and cookies and colors;
Long, long walks along the beach.
Clear head once again.
I envision my dreams in my mind
And plan to change it all.
Longer nights and shorter days;
September leaves as I put on my scarf,
Holding hands with the wind.
Thick socks and soup and music;
Red, brown, green leaves falling down.
Clear head once again.
I envision my love in my mind
And plan on changing it all.
Season of change, season of renewal,
Autumn is falling and I am excited.

Rivington St.

Crouched on my windowsill
Watching the movement under my feet
People walking, chatting, sitting, dancing,
Another police car. Music drifting along.
Regular noises, life.
I feel the need to cry tonight
But the tears won't fall.
You know what I want?
To be able to fall asleep anywhere
In my own place.
For the first time in my life.
I need crave want stability,
Me and my cat against all odds
Has been too long, too many months,
Years even.
The itchy-footed wanderer
Has found firm ground.
For now.
I'll always be around though,
Hovering above it all,
Watching through my splayed toes
And my cigarette smoke.

(Cruel) Summer

Cruel summer was on the lips of all the girls
Already back in June when the temperature rose
Now weeks have gone by and everything changed
I gave you up and opened my eyes again
She gave him another chance and closed up.
We danced around the open fires and laughed
We hugged each other so tightly, no letting go
But we all know how it will all go again
The days will get shorter, the colors will fade
The air will be crisper, and the sun will go down
The freedom we felt when we cried together
Will fade into the icy ground that I step on.
Remember how we said cruel summer?
How will we fare in the winter?
Can we huddle together and live through it as one?
I hope I hope I hope I hope I hope I hope I hope.

Breathe.

Music is Home

I

I sift through the oversized box, full of band shirts in different shapes of wear and tear, tour shirts with the date emblazoned on the back, women-sized shirts bought at merch stands, old, old shirts from decades ago, bought with money I scrimped and saved ahead of time. Widened neck holes, arms cut off, some teeny tiny that barely fit over these breasts I have since grown, kept out of nostalgia and memories and a faint hope that once my breastfeeding days subside I will comfortably fit in them again. Band names that no longer exist apart from in memories of basement bars and long nights, good looking guitarists always shredding my heart into pieces. The soft feel of the material between my fingers, the smell of bars and booze, Chanel no 19, coconut, and cold vodka still in my mind, conjured up through the long-lasting lavender softener scent.

II

Music you own me; you are the rhythm of my memories and haunt my future, hold me up and pull me down, bring me back and push me forward. The Siouxsie shirt that went from office stress to DJing til early in the morning at Midway, fence down low so the sunlight wouldn't bother us. Years gone by and I can still taste the air, jager and stolen kisses in the DJ booth up high, Bonnie Tyler for a laugh, the electric slide along the floor. The tiny Secret Machines shirt, so tiny I don't even know how it fit, fills my soul with a swaying happiness, because despite everything it was always going to be OK, right place and right time, a moment in time which would slip away from us, both moving along and thanking each other. The one Cure shirt from back in the day, proper vintage, a perfect gift from a perfect friend, a mutual love of The Cure framing a friendship, an appreciation of the deeper impact of music drilling it deeper.

III

The pale green Sonic Youth tee, the eye staring, knowing, watching, a time of sitting back and listening, observing and not participating, a time of sunshine and beaches and sobriety, where the drunken stories were no longer my own but those others told me. Barcelona wanderings leading me to moonlight ramblings from a balcony I will never see again, chain smoking with one hand, furiously writing with the other. The black Interpol t-shirt, purchased many, many years after my first Interpol show, that one in Staten Island, new to NYC, embracing my new life with an old but new friend, a door opening towards Ludlow and Orchard - Darkroom,

28

Motorcity, and then The Skinny and later 200 Orchard. Pianers on Sunday, and so much stomping up and down those streets, heels worn down on my Fryes, eyes bright with anticipation or ivresse or both. The first time I met them, these people I fell in love with through my headphones, I was shy and intimidated, and then it was just all home anyway. The streets, the people, the music. Interpol and Calla and Dead Combo, my Ludlow, maybe yours.

IV

Oh look there is my Spiritualized t-shirt, washed and worn so many times, so many memories of shows, Terminal 5, Radio City, Webster Hall... Hotel Rivington, watching the sun rise over the East River, a glass of red wine in my hand, having meaningful conversations with musicians, wishing I had more to offer, constantly feeling less than others, undermining my own value and feelings, a warrior fighting my own demons, while fighting my own self-worth. Spiritualized, weaving through my life, my firstborn's first show, a little secret in my womb, a pregnancy announcement whispered from one side of the balcony to the other. Come Together, before our lives all fell apart in an explosively wonderful manner. Spiritualized, always a cleansing, beautiful way to raise my soul, my happy music, sealing broken hearts, lifting me towards love. And always with my best friend, together even when we weren't. Surprisingly only one Nick Cave, my love now worn by my true life love, but so many moments in his presence from Lyon to the Beacon Theater, standing over me, that voice that transcends all others, whispering, goading, flipping your stomach inside out, grabbing you by the heart. There is no other, no other like him. The Kills, the one band I have seen more than any other, every time better than the last, never failing to grab me by the guts and shove me in front of my emotions.

V

And then there are those shirts that are only left in my memories, the original Ride the Lightning, paper thin with age, hash holes along the bottom, Metallica. I finally saw them 18 years later, Megadeth-Slayer-Metallica, teenage dreams coming alive in my 30's, jammed against the fence by the pit, screaming along to old songs with unknown new friends next to me. Strangers but together with the music. Seasons in the Abyss alive and well, lyrics taking me back to my teenage room in France, while standing on the soil of NYC. A 200 franc note blowing down the street, landing at my feet. I kept it for a week in case anyone claimed it and then ran to the shop in the center of town, spending half an hour deciding between two Nirvana shirts, finally opting for the one that wasn't the yellow smiley. My first own music t-shirt purchase, teenage uniform with my mismatched Doc Martens and ripped jeans. The Nine Inch Nails shirt, bought in the US on the Fragile tour, worn into the ground on a kibbutz in Israel, Trent's voice's effect on my heart lasting so much longer than his merch.

VI

Hundreds of shirts, all neatly folded in a box, all waiting to be worn again, telling the stories of a lifetime of music, of lifetimes of music, memories dancing to the beat of a drum, twirling towards a crescendo, caught in time. Right there, that high note, Leonard Cohen's smile as he dances across the stage; the smoke surrounding American X, still true today BRMC; Peter, white faced and dark-eyed, once again reunited with Daniel, David, and Kevin, and me standing from that balcony in the Times Square venue, wondering how I had finally managed to make a teenage Bauhaus dream come true. Red wine and Lit, running through the streets of NYC, places that now only exist in my memories and maybe yours. An unfinished story of places, people, and the music that brought us altogether.

Fighter Mode

From a distance my life has been a sequence of stepping stones, a skip, hop, or long jump to the next one, occasional moments where I fall into an abyss between stones, just to claw my way out again. There have also been many stones that have turned into tropical beaches, the peace of the waves washing over my toes while I bask in the warmth of the sun. Seasons sometimes clashed, sometimes rolled into each other seamlessly, yellow, brown, red on bright, bright blues and greens. Most of the time I am in fighter mode, standing strong but ready to kick back while protecting everything that is mine. "Mine" has never been something concrete, but rather intangible: my life, everything that I have built with my own two hands and feet, my love, my family…

Nowadays I am not alone, having found another fighter like me, both more tranquil together than we ever were alone. We have created this beautiful little family, 5 of us now, little fighters just like their parents. Most days I stand strong, protective, mother bear to what is mine. But some days I feel weary, feet heavy, plodding rather than skipping. My legs aren't so graceful anymore, dancing over the spaces in time, more sturdy, more mare less foal. This week my eyes feel heavy, every gesture is calculated, foggy, a chore. I dream of a hot bubble bath, toes splayed in the water, singing Tracy Chapman and dreaming of beaches. Can I make this happen faster this beach dream? What more can we do to get there? These are the days when I listen to myself speak and it doesn't sound right, I am on a business call and I know I sound genuine, but in reality it's all forced. There are days that I wonder about the damage I did to myself working in a place that was the opposite of my essence, shoving a cone into a hexagon and crossing my fingers it wouldn't look fake. By night it was boots on the bar downing Stoli rocks and feeling at home, by day it was frantic typing and responding and troubleshooting, pretending, pretending, pretending. Even now, 6 years later I feel that anxiety, the need to respond right away. I tell myself it's all right, and then I forget to respond altogether.

Apparently the middle ground isn't my strong point.

Too Soon

A child smiles up at you
Pure happiness for a second.
The innocence, the incomprehension, the pure need to learn.
A child is a child, there are no boundaries,
No differences. Color, religion. Comparisons certainly.
One year old, wide-open eyes, tears fall easily, but
A smile comes even faster.
A group of individuals, bent on hatred.
No care for talk, for cease-fires, for peace.
The world is violence, shock and terror.
But those who believe it are those who care not to look,
They are on the bottom stairs of the pyramid...
Up, up, up the heads are seated.
Preaching and condemning, teaching the lies.
Talks of martyrdom, of heavens, of God's will.
The country will be ours! We butcher and we lurk.
They prepare and believe, they have given themselves
The right to kill and maim.
Just look at their eyes, wild with bloodshed.
But the child is oblivious to the world,
The child is not the cause of suffering.
They never self-examine, never look, never listen.
That child never decided to die,
But the member of the group did.
One is a choice, one is murder.

You (bang the drums)

Vodka nights and cocaine dreams,
Past, present, future all in uproar,
Meld together, forget don't live.
You and me, together forever in a moment
I forgot it all; And then all over again.
Same place, same time, another moment.
All one long twist of moments,
Somehow together, mainly unlinked.
How wrong but how right, how wrong.
I miss your eyes, but never those moments.

Oh those bells...

Another morning of church bells
Jangling away in my head
Doom bells clashing with the snow's party
Softly falling on my face
Against the icy wind I brace my heart
There is no clearance, there is no sale
Future is an everyday option
What appeared to be a good idea
Last night
Is today's worst enemy, source of anger
Always the same question, chanting along
With the incessant ring of the bells
Why oh why oh why oh why
As soon as the snowflake falls to the ground
It soaks up the dirt of the street
Sparkling for a while, lights going dim
Until all that is left is grey mush
But the church still stands, snow, rain, sun
The bells never go rusty, always oiled
They just never fail or fall aground.

Sláinte

What do you want from the menu?
You. Only you.
Eyes.
Those eyes.
Sometimes I didn't understand you,
I know I was hard to read too.
Scared.
I can still hear that sound, the cracking,
All the way down.
It continued to beat long afterwards.
And I sewed myself back together,
One bloody stitch at a time.

Fear drowned in Powers,
Words propped up by Guinness,
And feelings straight from the heart.

Life changed.
Love changed.

You came back and I disappeared.
For the best.
Yes, for the best.

Beautiful beautiful blue eyes
Time to say goodbye
I will leave silently
Otherwise I will never go.

I'm not going to be just another Ludlow St statistic.

Chosen One

Fuzzy eyes
It's all dark and the music is on
We giggle
Oh it sounds like Front 242
It is Front 242 silly

You are as pale as whole milk
I'm hazy
Drunk
High
Fragile.
Sitting in the back garden,
Smoking, watching the sun rise.
I didn't realize I was the chosen one
Until you chose another.

Mariposa de la Noche

Dance
Dance
Dance
You are twirling with abandon,
Mouth hovering between smile and scream,
Black and white with a little grey
Sing
Sing
Sing
Words fall into the abyss,
Colorful images collecting in a puddle,
Fading in the moonlight.
Love
Love
Love
Silence kills the words,
Ethereal touch disappears into the mirror,
Butterfly moth once again,
Darkness. A stream of light.
Gone.

Light

The star lit up her eyes
Dimmed down, messed up, ready;
Legs spread around his torso
Sweat mingles in time with the beat
It's hot hot hot hot hot.
Torch it down.
The lights have gone out,
I like to touch, to feel;
It's all good now.
Upside down I'm smiling,
Grinning against everything.
Black, dark, full and open;
I will be my own light
I will lead my own way,
Laughing, crying, spitting, screaming.

Like two solitary
Rocks drawn together
By flowers that grow despite
The despair that remains
Stagnant all around.

Consolidating the Foundations

I

The mirror doesn't ever lie these days. Where once nights without sleep gave me a hollowed-eye, slightly rock chic look, now they provide a puffier, ringed with black circles stare, tiny lines sprouting from all corners. I am often swimming in seas of the past, stopping off on islands and rocks to ruminate over strings left untied, that I sometimes forget to look at myself in the now. More and more frequently I catch myself in the middle of an action, in the center of a thought process, and suddenly wonder when the last time I thought of me was. Of me here now.

II

My past needs to be written, and so many words left unsaid, so many phrases still hanging there, suspended in time. But my present needs to be remembered too, as a whole, more than a day to day endeavor. I live in my present so deeply, but so deeply as a mother, a friend, a daughter, a sister, a partner, that I start to use all those layers as a protective coat, forgetting that the core needs to breathe too. Is this motherhood? Do we always forget to breathe? At what point do we realize that we need to go first sometimes? Just sometimes.

III

This tiredness goes beyond simple children waking at night fatigue, beyond certain levels of sleep deprivation; it comes from a feeling of slight hopelessness, feet stuck in quick-drying concrete, fingers holding onto crumbling rock above an abyss. There is the everyday, the life at home which often uplifts, sometimes wearies, and is somewhat comforting in its mélange of routine and impulsive dance parties. And then there is the rest of the world, the one I need to send my children out into, where they will have to answer questions about race and religion and beliefs, where often what they will be taught will counter what we talk about at home. And then even further than down the street are the bombs and the threats, humans fighting other humans, humans massacring the planet without regard. How can we consolidate the beauty of nature and also of man-made art and creations with the heap of steaming muck that we are also to blame for? Here lies my fatigue, my sadness, my unwillingness to remove the protective layers of filler, because without them I don't know how much strength I will have to fight the battles. My children give me so much more willpower to fight for change. I made the choice to have children and this erases my right to wallow in selfish self-doubt and aimless direction. But at the same time I must remember that strength and power are to be nurtured and given time to grow, and growth comes from the core, from within, as well as from those we let in.

IV

I tell my little ones, especially my eldest who deals with severe anxiety, to calm down and breathe every day, something that I should probably be doing more frequently too. Head against the cold front of the refrigerator door, eyes closed for a few seconds, listen to the sound of the ocean, swish swash, in your ears and breathe. Once again, breathe. Put your hand over your heart and feel the beat slow down to a gentle cadence, a walk instead of a gallop. We don't have anywhere to be, not right now, there is no rush. In a way we have all the time in the world. Actually I want us just to have all the time in the world. A simpler life, one rid of the constant hustle, where we can stop to listen to the wind as it blows through the valley, and not hesitate to run down to the water to dip our toes into it. I don't mind certain hardships when the background and the foundations make them easier to bear. Having little money is easier on the mind when one can cook food grown from the garden, collect eggs from the chickens clucking in the yard. Freezing winters are calming when snow covers the land and you can sit in front of the fire, hot chocolate and warm lights. Boiling summers are different when the ocean is just steps away, with cliff sides offering shelter and secret caves. And so on, there are ways to make even the simplest of lives fulfilling, an aspiration that will never leave me.

"Not everyone's strength is your strength"

Home that was never home

Almond trees and chattering squirrels,
Purring of the AC unit behind my head,
Faint sounds of cars in the distance.
Warm sun on my toes and
That familiar smell of California.

Home that was never home.

Freeways, smoking in the car, singing,
Old friends, new faces, everything so big.
No tension: I have space,
No constant noise: I can think.

Home that was never home.

Two thousand five hundred and fifty eight
Miles across the country to my

Home that was never home.

I never miss you.
I never think of you.
But you will always be here so warm and friendly and familiar.

Home that was never home.

There are now two separate hearts beating inside my body. Insane, amazing, strange, wonderful, frightening, and so calmly beautiful.

Home Plus Heart

I was born in the land of hope and glory,
And lived for many years amongst
Liberté, Egalité, Fraternité.
My roots are here and there
Scattered but firmly established,
I think.
I went to the land of milk and honey
And lived for many months amongst
Sabras, tradition, and love.
Now I dream of going back home
Where my roots are calling me,
Come home.

Where you go I shall lead -
I must follow my heart.

Believe

All I see is people telling me
What to wear
How to look
Who to be.
But I am Me.
I believe in Me.
I believe in Me.

I don't care for your
Hair Clothes Body
Advice.
I don't care for your
Perfectly perfected
Perfection.

I care for the tangible
Warmth; Touch; Reality.

I believe in Me.
I believe in Me.

Pure

Sleeping baby, so quiet in my arms
Clenched fist around my finger,
I dare not remove it in case you wake up
These moments are soft
Hazy, mesmerizing.
I feel the heaviness behind my eyes
Days of little sleep building up
Sorry, nights. I dream, eyes open.
The book falls to the ground
On the same page I left it an hour ago.
These moments, too short
I forget to appreciate them fully
These moments where I do no wrong.

You Said Wait and See

Shut up silly woman
Scaremongerer
You read too much fiction
It's OK, you are white.
Don't worry
You are the right kind of immigrant.
And then all of a sudden
5 year olds in handcuffs
11 month old babies ripped from their mothers' arms
Friends lose jobs
Others hide behind stone-cold statues;
We march and we talk and we resist,
Apparently we are liars
And probably traitors.
A wall goes up
Stifling us, but that is freedom of speech
It only goes one way
YOU can speak
But I can't, not me, immigrant, woman, multi-ethnic child creator.

Waiting

Waiting, waiting...
I hear her screaming in the background, wondering why I am not coming back
I abandoned her. For 30 minutes. A meeting.
Is it worth all that heartbreak, for 30 minutes?
My heart splinters at the sound, how long will she need me this much?
Mum back? Mum back?
Of course I am coming back.
I will never leave.
But that crying, that crying, it tears me apart every time.
I don't even know what to say to her to make it better.
Motherhood. There is always an underlying fear, right there.

Goodbye bitterness and anger, I let you go
Welcome home girl, this is where you live
No one will stop me from being who I am
Because that is who I love
And ultimately who you love too.

It's a win-win game we play
No going back now, just going home.

An Epiphany

An epiphany of some sorts, rich layers of words that I want to peel apart slowly, submerging myself in their beauty. I've made it back home again, my first love never loses the ability to cloak me in a protective blanket, rainbow-hued, dense with images. I read with one hand and write with the other, inspired. There she is, the beacon I've been looking for.

I can now turn around and observe the past instances of Jade, each one donning a new layer, protecting the inner child, evolving. The quiet me, the anxious me, the one who traveled to a new country in search of home me, and who did it over and over again; the angry me, the one who tried to conform, and the one who stood out. The stomping me and the tiptoeing me, twirling en pointe around the potholes me, using caution tape as a blindfold. How can it be so easy to view life as a movie reel? A sequence of court métrages, credits disappearing into a past that will not let itself be forgotten.

This book I am reading has the artistic depth of a handmade Persian rug, each stitch exquisitely attached to the next, a story woven between other stories; a life infused into the wool, into the imagery. My mind starts to wander; I imagine my fingers tracing lines in the warm, damp sand: you are here, you are now. You are here, you are now, but you still keep tugging the strings of the past along behind you. Tin cans rattling along the shoreline, a "just married" trail, because yes, all instances of me are married together into one. Bang, bang, bang down the stairs they go behind me, the racket loud enough to send spiders scurrying to safety and for my brain to cloud. There is no more Stoli to clear the air, no more Powers to shush the noises. They are collecting dust in the corners, relegated to a shelf in my past, my fingers sometimes caressing their cool glass shell, the smell familiar in my nostrils, tantalizing, then gone. Away, I pushed you away.

The rain is pouring tonight, tapping on the floor of the balcony upstairs and dripping through the open roof by the stairwell. The ground is too dry to soak the water, I picture it running into the streets, overwhelming drains, soaking through to the tents. Haphazard creations of old sheets and tarps, our homeless left alone out there in the dark; wet, and forgotten. Rain is my noise-cancelling savior, a more sane version of booze, but for those left behind it is damp, mold, and unfair. The bootstraps long since rotted away in the deserts far away, where rain rarely falls but rot happens anyway.

That is the me now, and the me of before, pulled in two directions, one of comfort and one of pain, my empathy for others always sleeping with one eye open, my protective barrier with eyes at half mast, alert and poised. I worry too much. My worries run deep, etched in those lines along my forehead, creased, fraught. Each element zaps the next, a ball of high current worry, a ball I carry on my back, protecting it from touching anyone else. Its static is sparkling, random cracks in the dry air. Maybe the rain will ease her for a while, dampen her spirits, let me let go. When did I become so goddamn serious? I miss my laughter, that deep sound from the belly, that giggle what won't stop, that rolling around the floor I can't breathe laughter. Why do I hide her, afraid if set her free I will discover that all of these strings I tie around everything are unnecessary? I miss her, so natural and spontaneous, I miss her.

As my thoughts wander, roam, the book falls from my hands, the pen stays poised in the air, a drip of black ink staining my fingers. The book is my own, the tapestry of words created inside my own mind, inspired but I still   doubt   myself.

Tomorrow I will laugh. Tomorrow I will be spontaneous again.

Vivre et non pas survivre.

Bring me the summer rain and match it with the autumn moon and it will be just like the heavens are smiling down on you with happiness.

Us

Home is
You Me
Us Them
Our hands touch comfortably,
Comforting. Broken together,
We love, we live, we plan.
Home is
Us Together,
Hand in hand through
The mud, the lakes, the sand,
Over
Mountains and patched up ladders,
Under
Iron bridges and giant buildings.
Home is this love,
Phenomenal in its normalcy
I love
You
Me
Us
Them.
My family is my home.

ABOUT THE AUTHOR

Jade Anna Hughes was born in Rutland, England, grew up in Grenoble, France, spent over a decade pounding the streets of New York City in search of stories, oblivion and hope, and now lives in sunny Northern California with her other half and three children. Jade has been writing since she can remember and blogs on a regular basis on From the Inside, her own creation, as well as several other publications. She also works as a freelance writer, creating content for other people to use to their hearts content.

This is her first collection of poetry. Her collection of essays on motherhood, With Spring Comes Hope, is also currently available.